Celebrated Christm

2)

7 Christmas Favorites Arranged for Early Intermediate Pianists

Robert D. Vandall

The Christmas recital is the most popular one in my wife's and my studio. We schedule three short Christmas recitals each year so that all of the students who wish to perform are included. The arrangements in *Celebrated Christmas Solos, Book 3,* are for students at the early-intermediate level. The carols and songs chosen are those most favored by students, as they love playing carols and songs that they know well. Short introductions and codas extend the arrangements into satisfying musical experiences. It is my hope that students will enjoy playing, teachers will enjoy teaching, and audiences will enjoy hearing these arrangements. After all, Christmas music captures the essence of the Christmas season! Merry Christmas!

Robert D. Vandall

Contents

ISBN 0-7390-4340-4

God Rest Ye Merry, Gentlemen

English Carol
Arr. by Robert D. Vandall

...udents to become
...ght-reading or

...ly in common time
...inger positions in C and G,
...gain confidence before moving
on to bass clef. It then sets the same standard for bass clef before moving on to both hands.

The second and third books pick up where the previous left off and get progressively more difficult as you work your way through them. Each of these has a second section comprised of music from the Classical repertoire. There are some time signatures and rhythmic figures that are different than those in the first section. If you are unfamiliar with these, they are covered thoroughly in Rhythm and Meter for All Musicians, available at:

www.RobertAnthonyPublishing.com.

A good strategy is to read a few pages per day, continuing where you left off the previous day. If the material becomes too difficult for your skill level, start again at the beginning and you should be able to get further in the book the second time through. Continue on in this fashion until you have reached the end.

The goal is to read the music, not to memorize the songs. It is very important to keep changing the material by continuing through the book instead of repeating the same material each day.

Music Reading Skills for Piano

Level 1

www.RobertAnthonyPublishing.com

Circle of Fifths

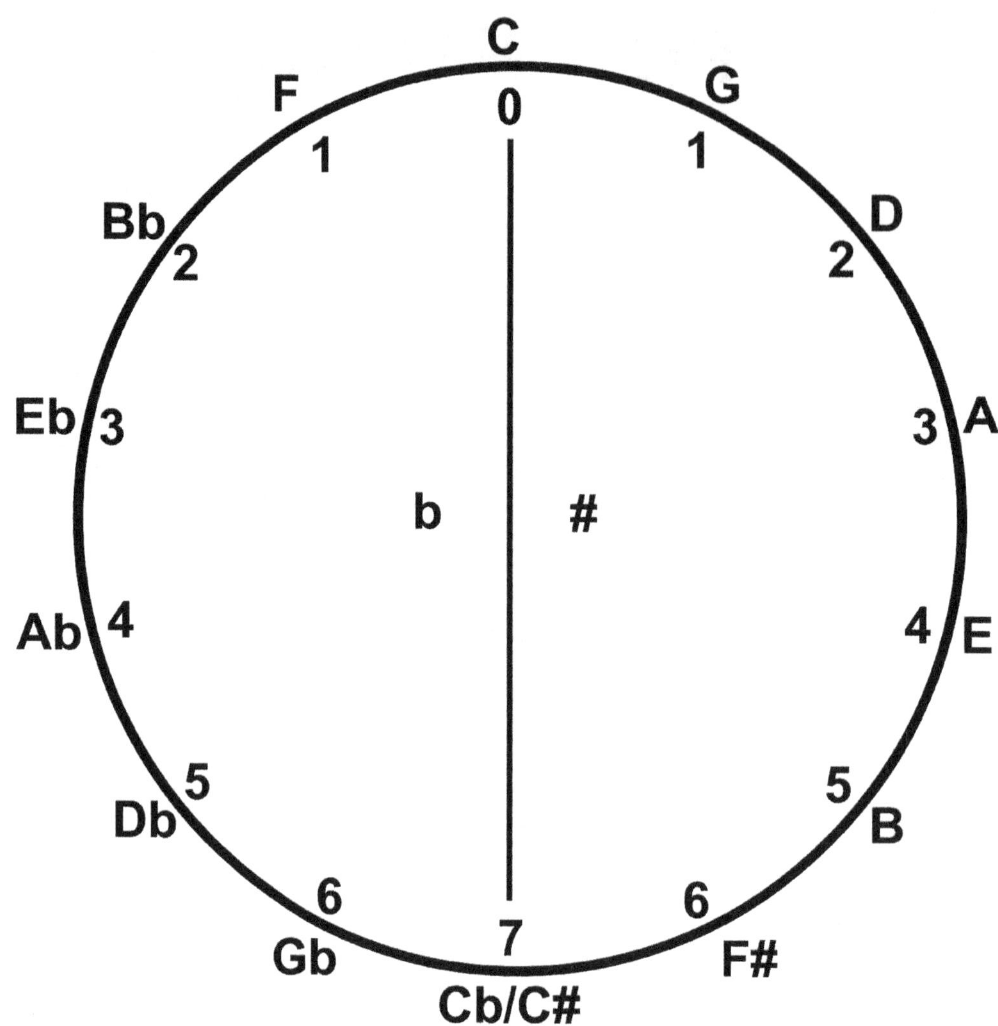

You can use the Circle of Fifths to recognize key signatures by how many sharps (#) or flats (b) are in the key. The key of A Major has three sharps, for example, and the key of Bb has two flats. In the key signatures, sharps always occur in the order: F C G D A E B, while flats always occur in the opposite order: B E A D G C F.

The following sentence will help you to memorize these orders:

Frank's Cat Got Drunk At Elmo's Bar

Basic Rhythm and Counting

The reading exercises in this book are all in 4/4 time, also called common time. In common time, there are four beats per measure.

Below are examples of how to count the different note types that are used.

Whole notes receive four beats:

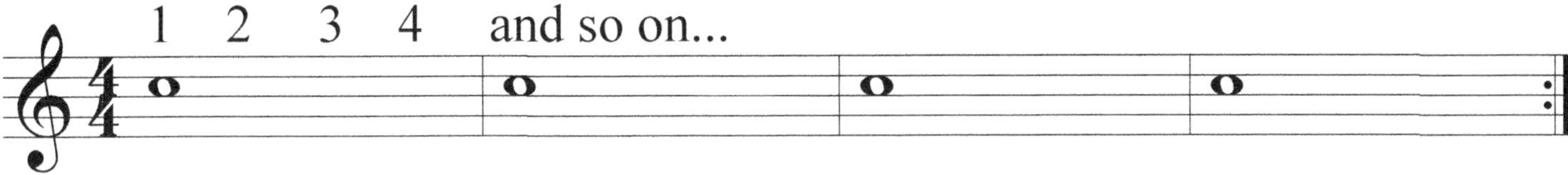

Half notes receive two beats:

Quarter notes receive one beat:

Eighth notes receive half a beat:

Identifying Note Names in Treble Clef

Traditional Approach

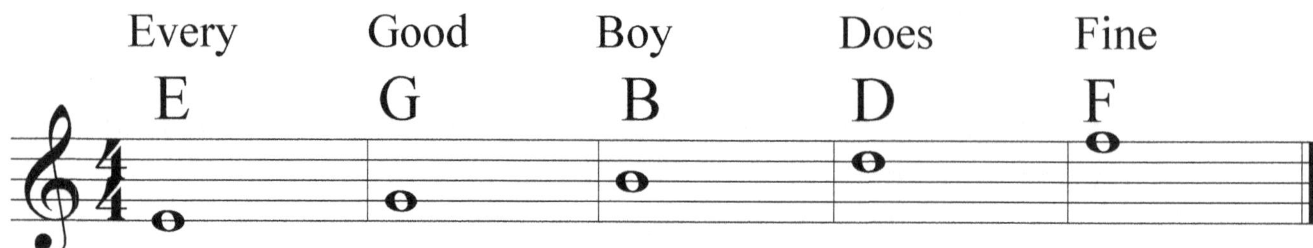

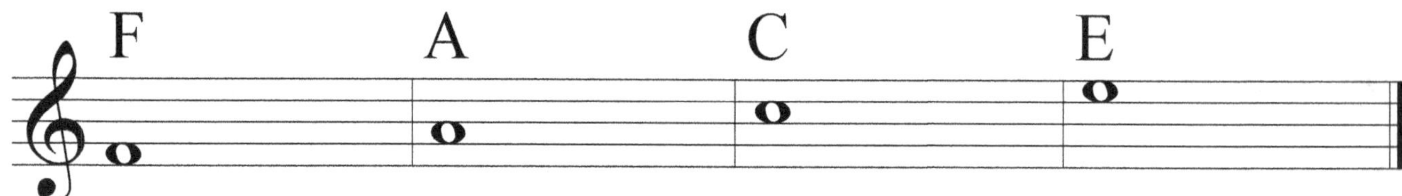

While the traditional approach above is helpful, you will likely find it to be even more helpful to know that the musical alphabet (A-G) ascends the lines and spaces of the staff that the notes are written on.

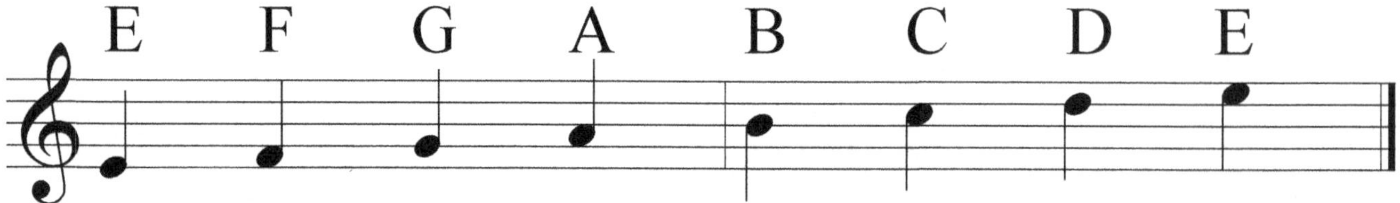

Ledger Lines: Notes written beyond the lines and spaces of the staff appear on additional lines called ledger lines.

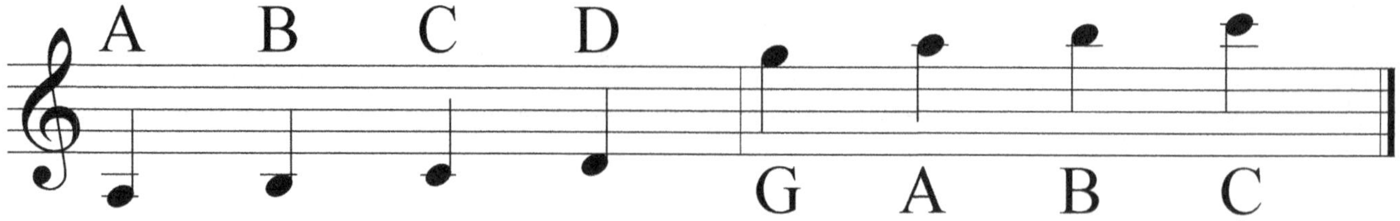

Identifying Note Names in Bass Clef

Traditional Approach

All A | Cars C | Eat E | Gas G

While the traditional approach above is helpful, you will likely find it to be even more helpful to know that the musical alphabet (A-G) ascends the lines and spaces of the staff that the notes are written on.

Ledger Lines: Notes written beyond the lines and spaces of the staff appear on additional lines called ledger lines.

C Position for the Right Hand

Reading Exercises 1-10 are written to be played by the right hand in C Position. The right hand's thumb (1) is to be placed on "middle C". Middle C is the C that is nearest to center on a piano. Use the diagram on the next page to place your right hand on the keyboard: thumb on middle C and one finger per white key thereafter.

C Position

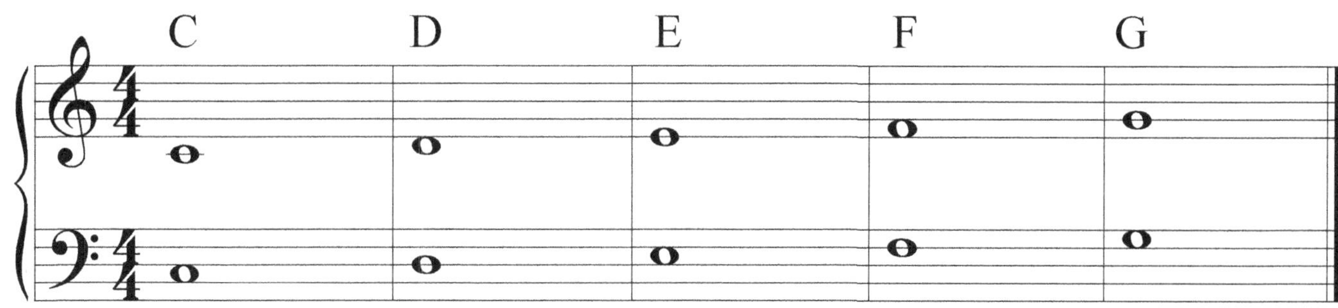

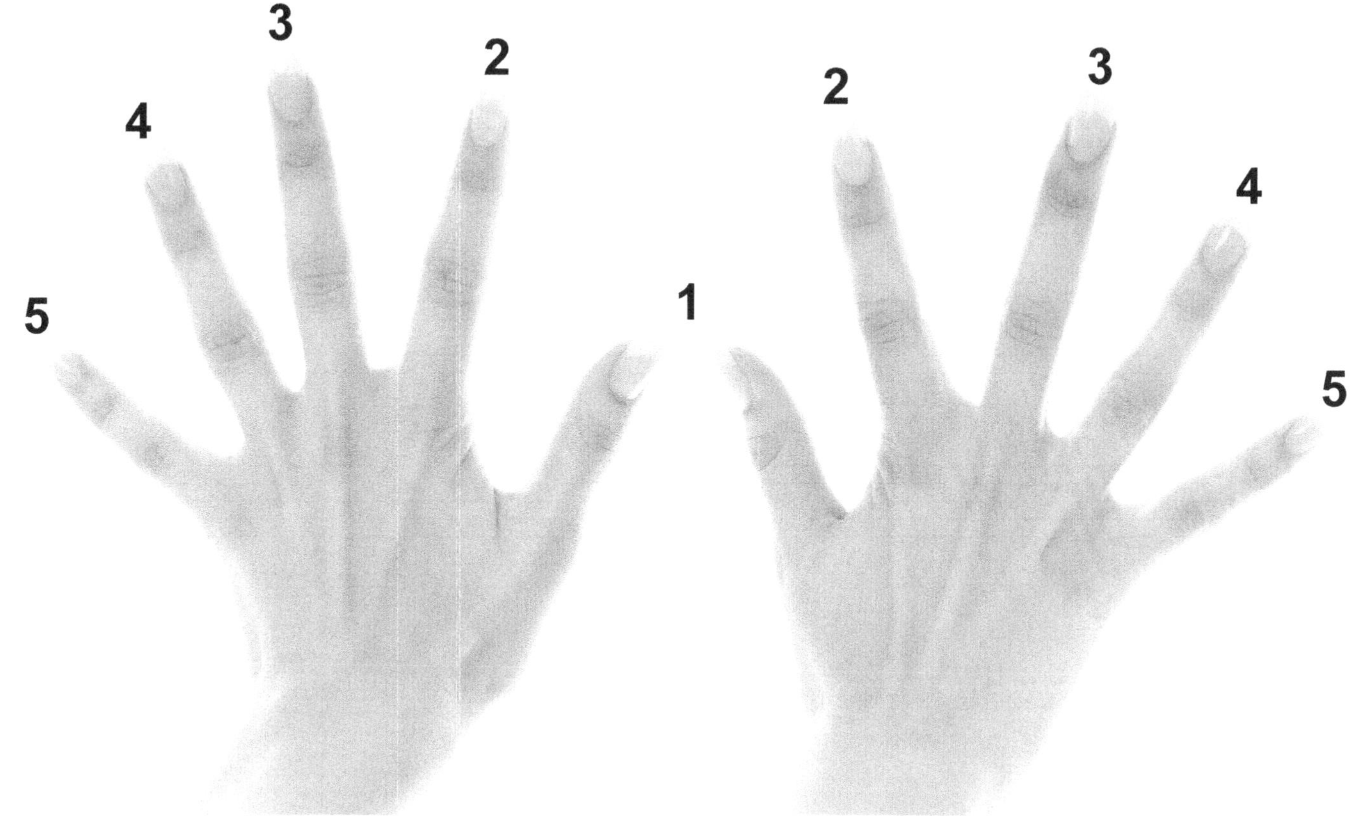

1

2

3

4

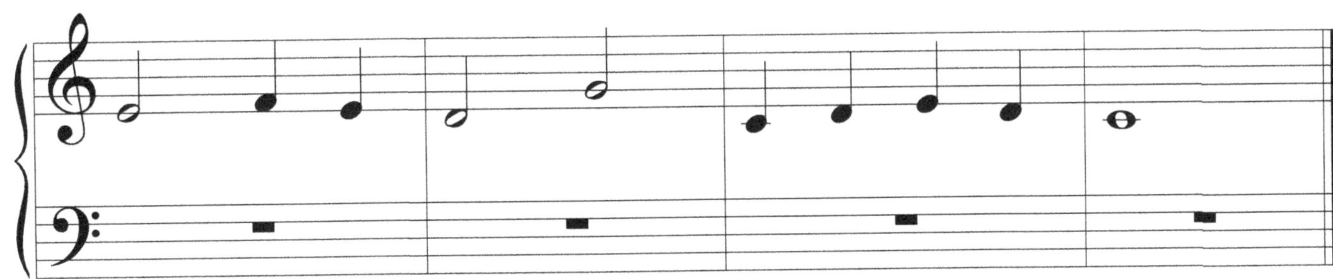

5

6

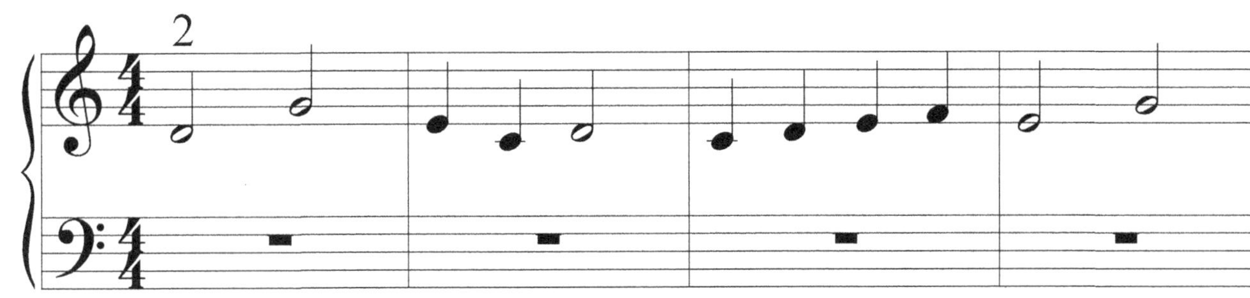

7

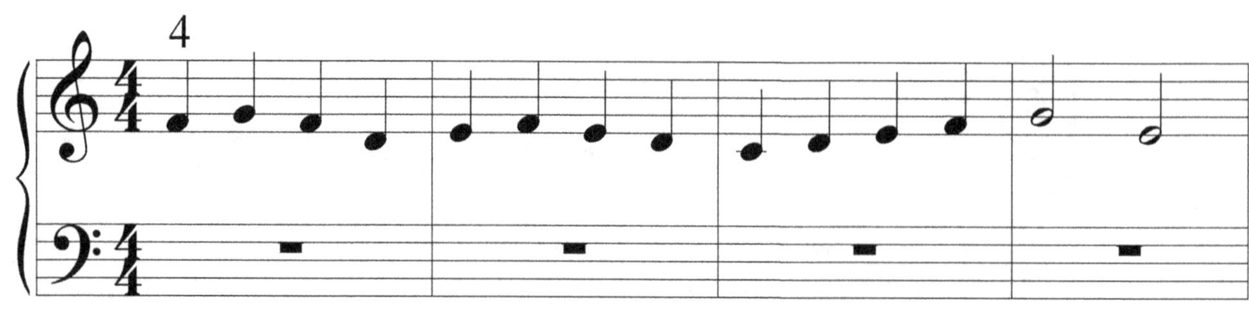

8

9

10

G Position for the Right Hand

Reading Exercises 11-20 are written to be played by the right hand in G Position. The right hand's thumb (1) is to be placed on the G immediately higher than "middle C". Use the diagram on the next page to place your right hand on the keyboard: thumb on the appropriate G and one finger per white key thereafter.

G Position

G A B C D

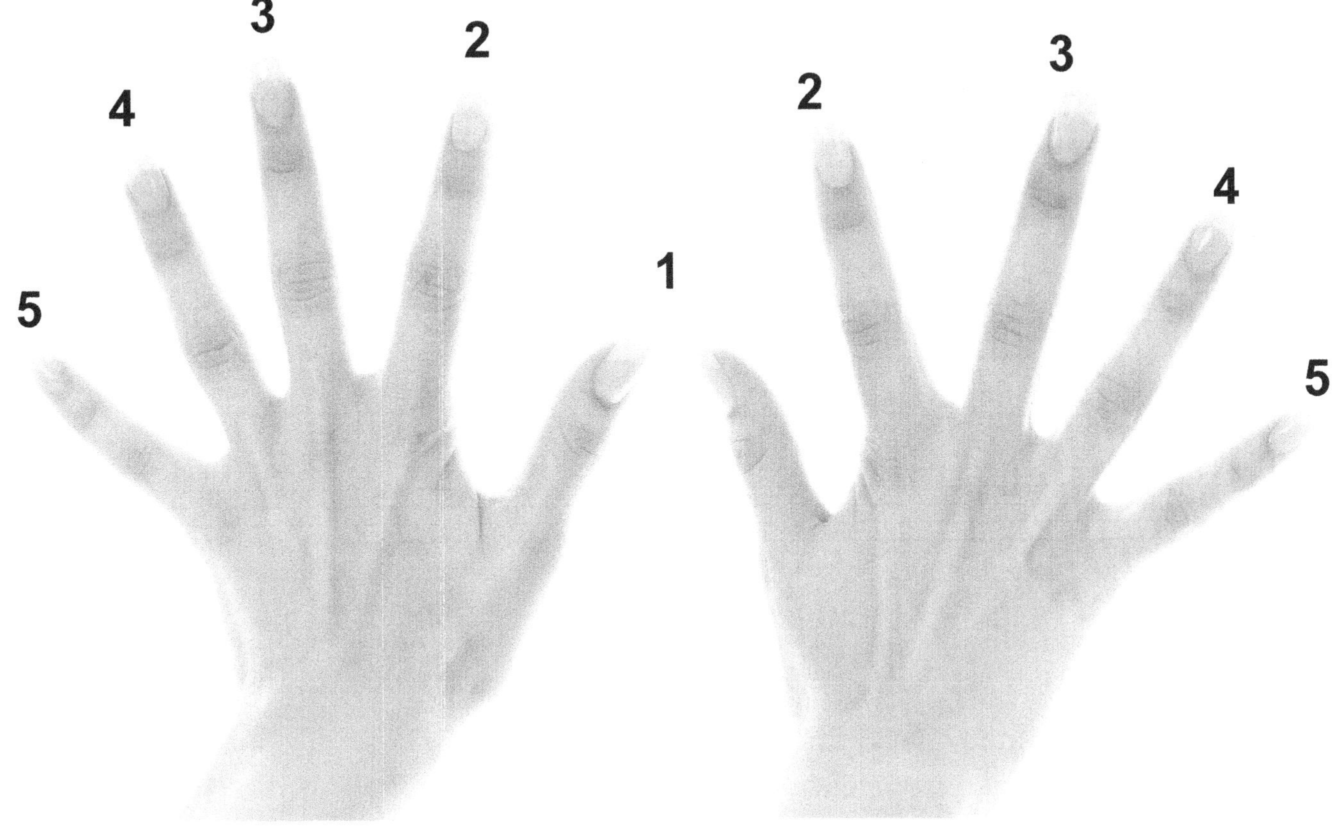

11

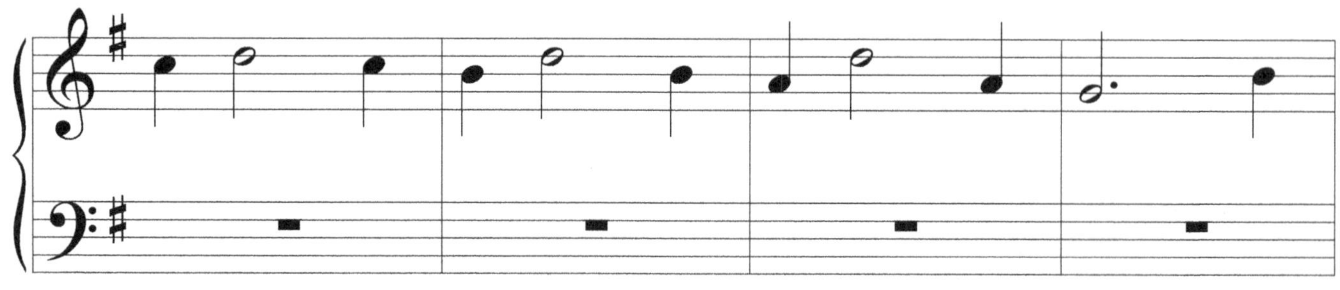

12

13

14

15

16

17

18

19

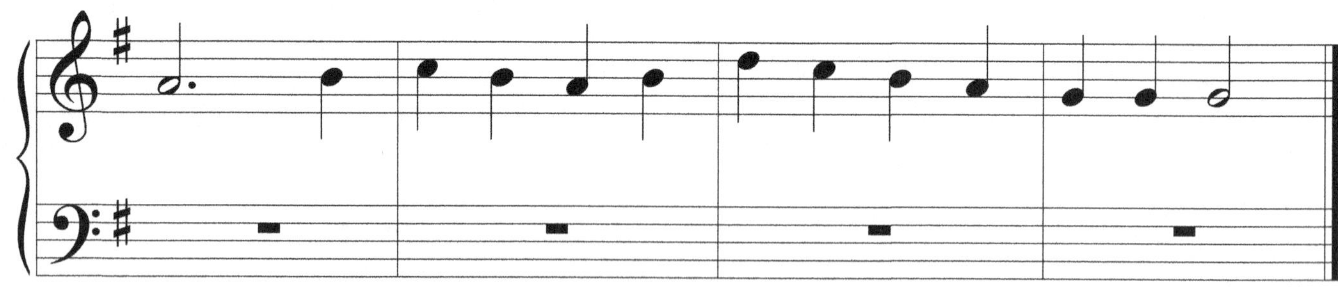

20

C Position for the Left Hand

Reading Exercises 21-30 are written to be played by the left hand in C Position. The left hand's little finger (5) is to be placed on the C one octave lower than "middle C". Use the diagram on the next page to place your left hand on the keyboard: little finger on the appropriate C and one finger per white key thereafter.

C Position

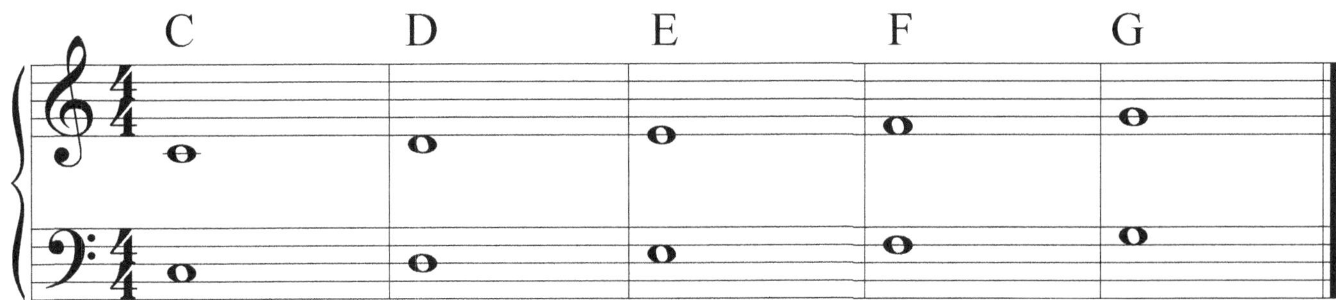

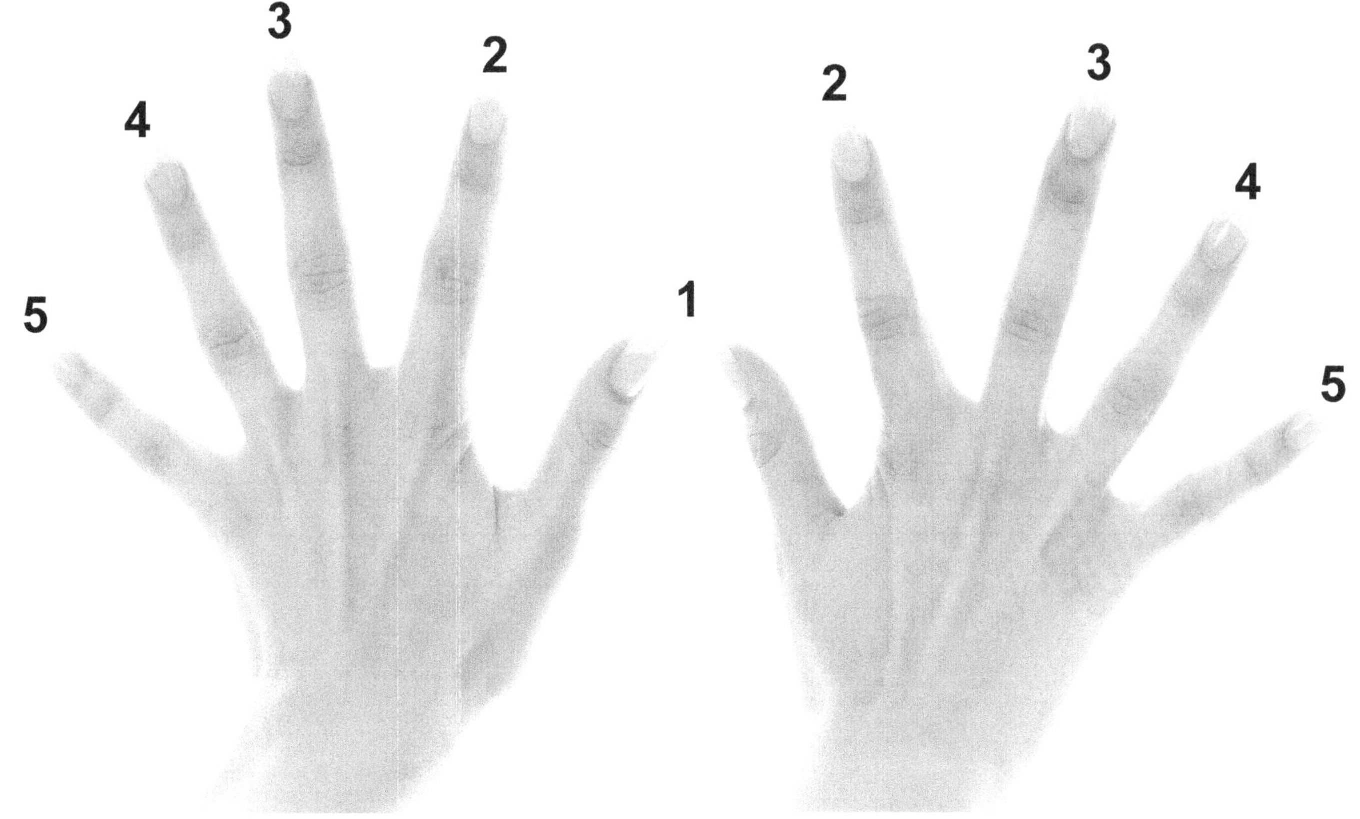

21

22

23

24

25

26

27

28

29

30

G Position for the Left Hand

Reading Exercises 31-40 are written to be played by the left hand in G Position. The left hand's little finger (5) is to be placed on the G immediately lower than "middle C". Use the diagram on the next page to place your left hand on the keyboard: little finger on the appropriate G and one finger per white key thereafter.

G Position

G A B C D

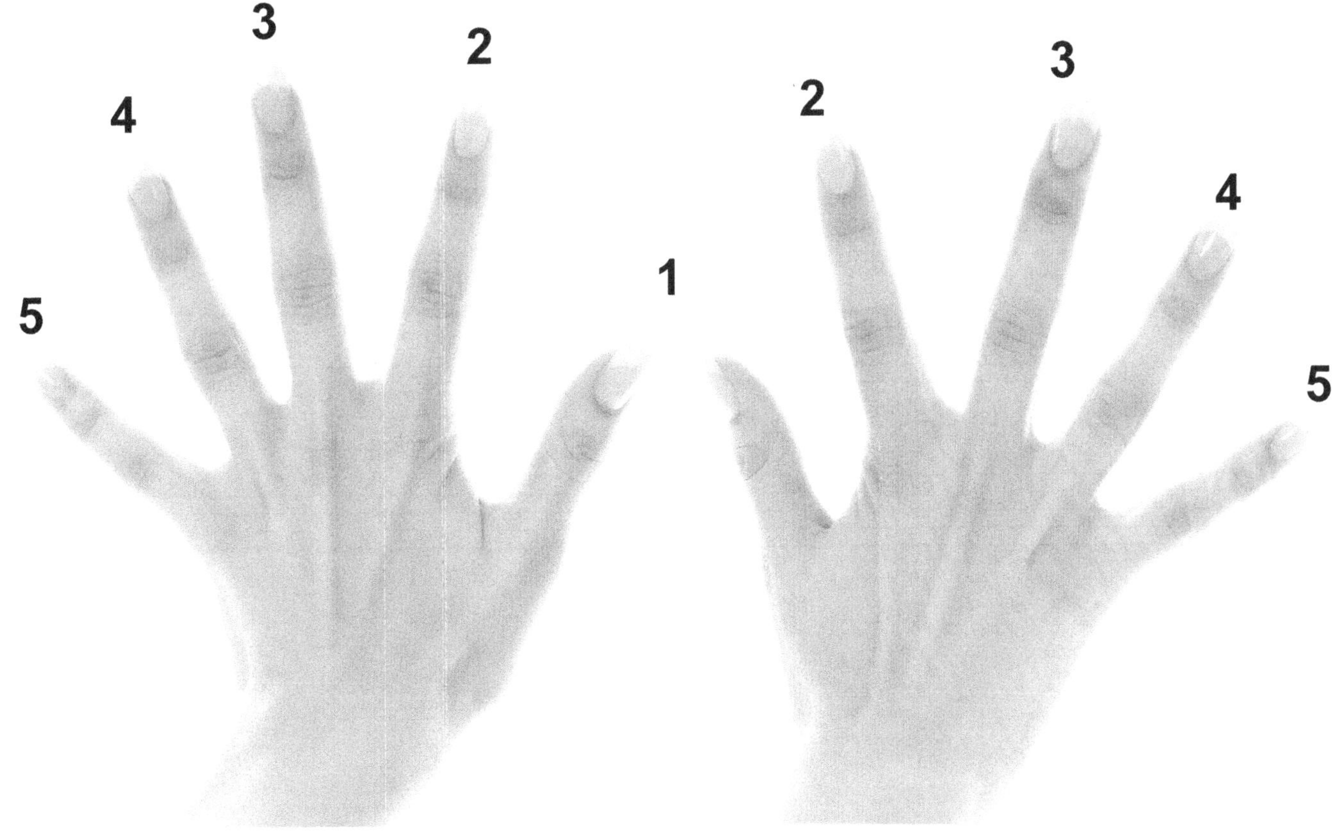

31

32

33

34

35

36

37

38

39

40

C Position for the Both Hands

Exercises 41-50 are to be played with both hands in C position. Use the diagram on the next page to place your hands on the keyboard. By now, you should be quite familiar with what "C position" means. You can review the previous sections on C position if needed.

C Position

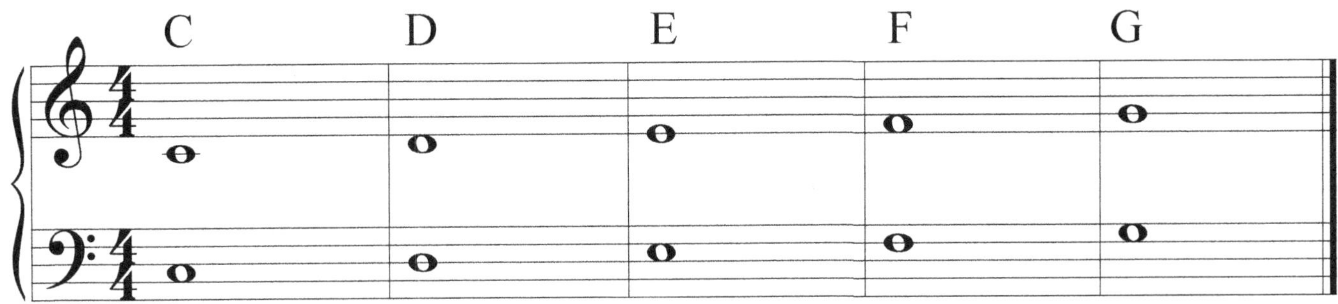

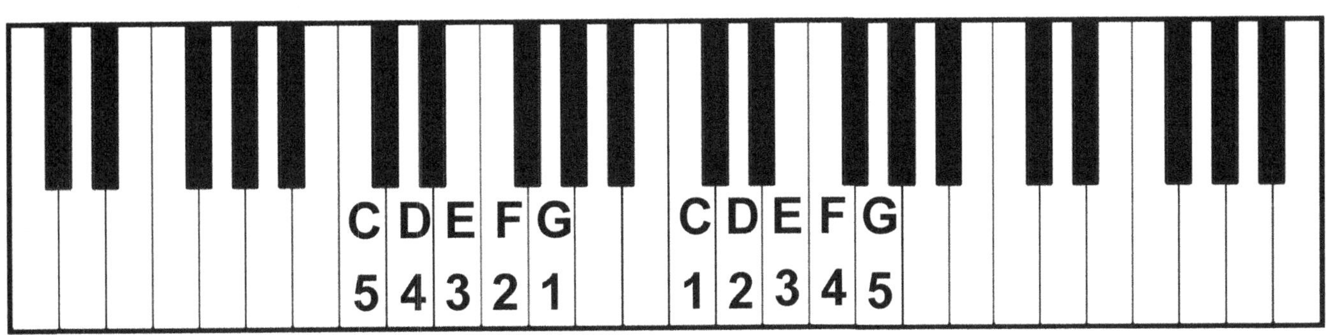

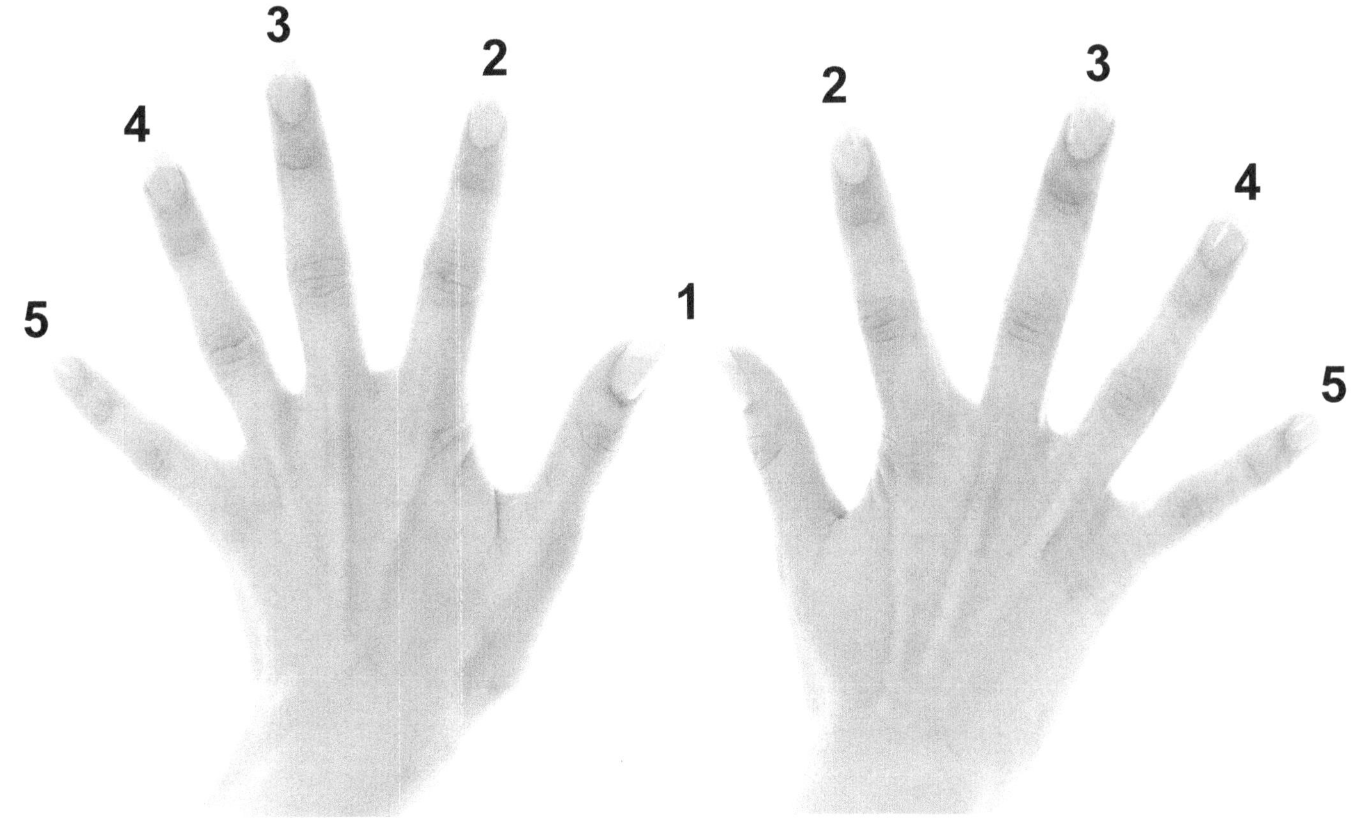

41

42

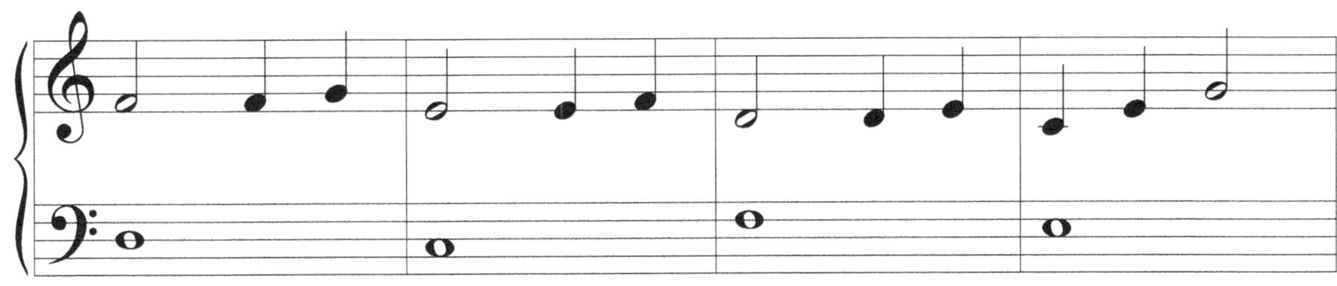

43

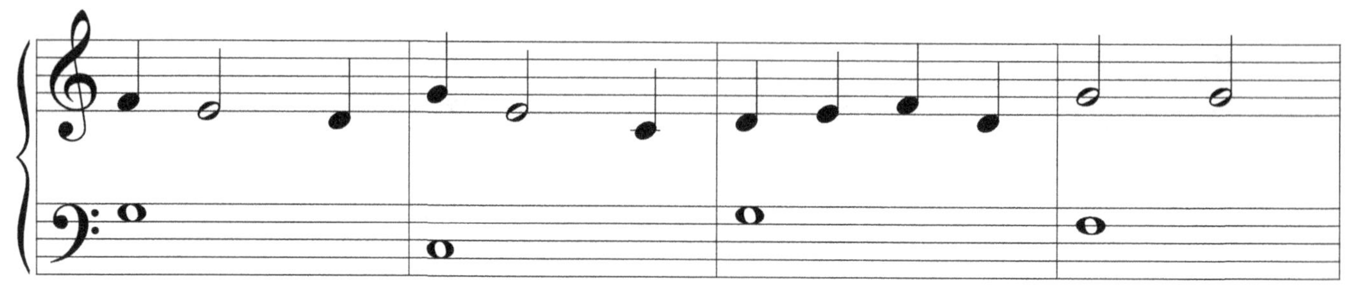

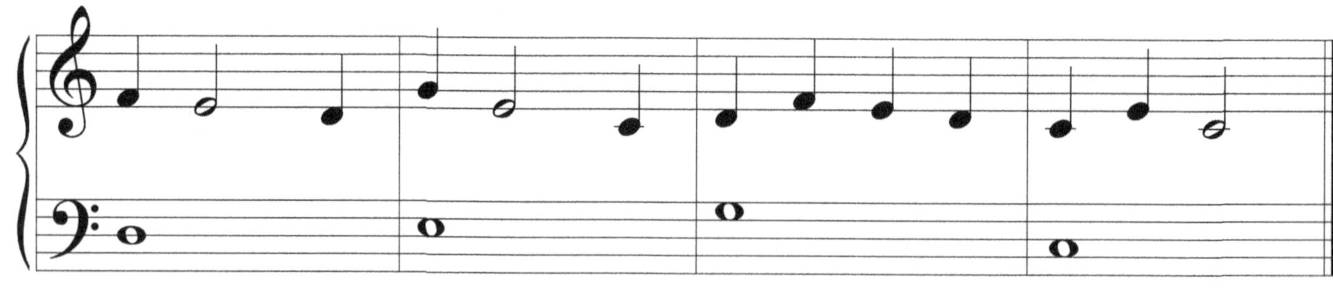

44

45

46

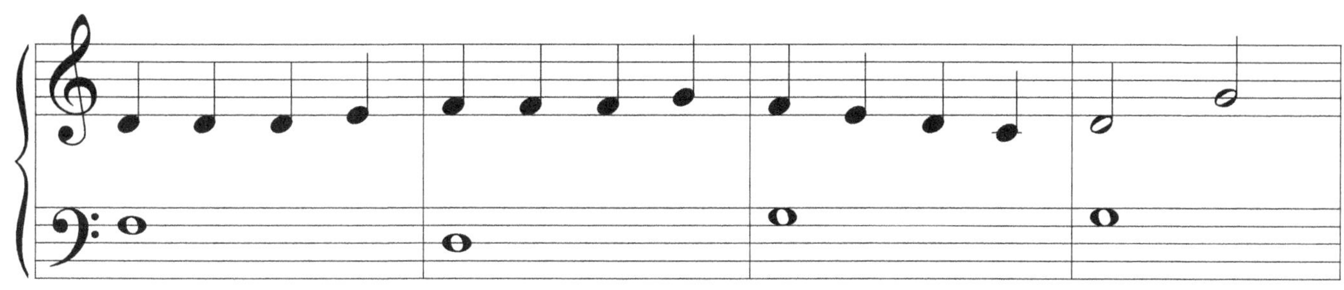

47

48

49

50

G Position for the Both Hands

Exercises 51-60 are to be played with both hands in G position. Use the diagram on the next page to place your hands on the keyboard. By now, you should be quite familiar with what “G position” means. You can review the previous sections on G position if needed.

G Position

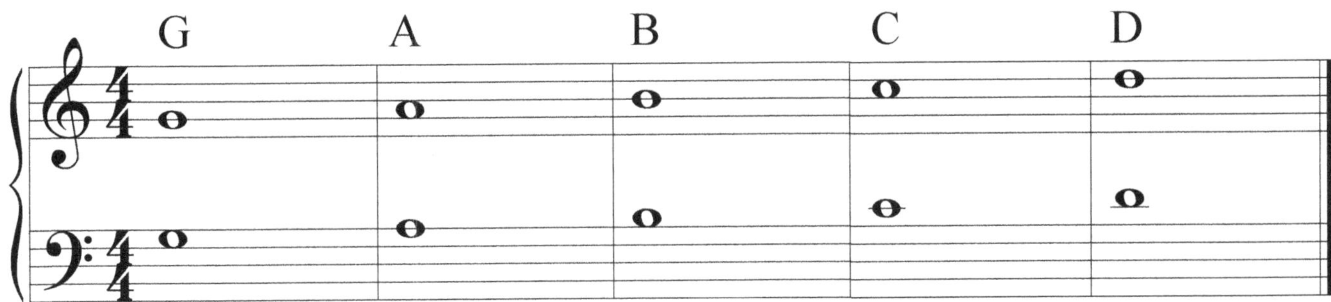

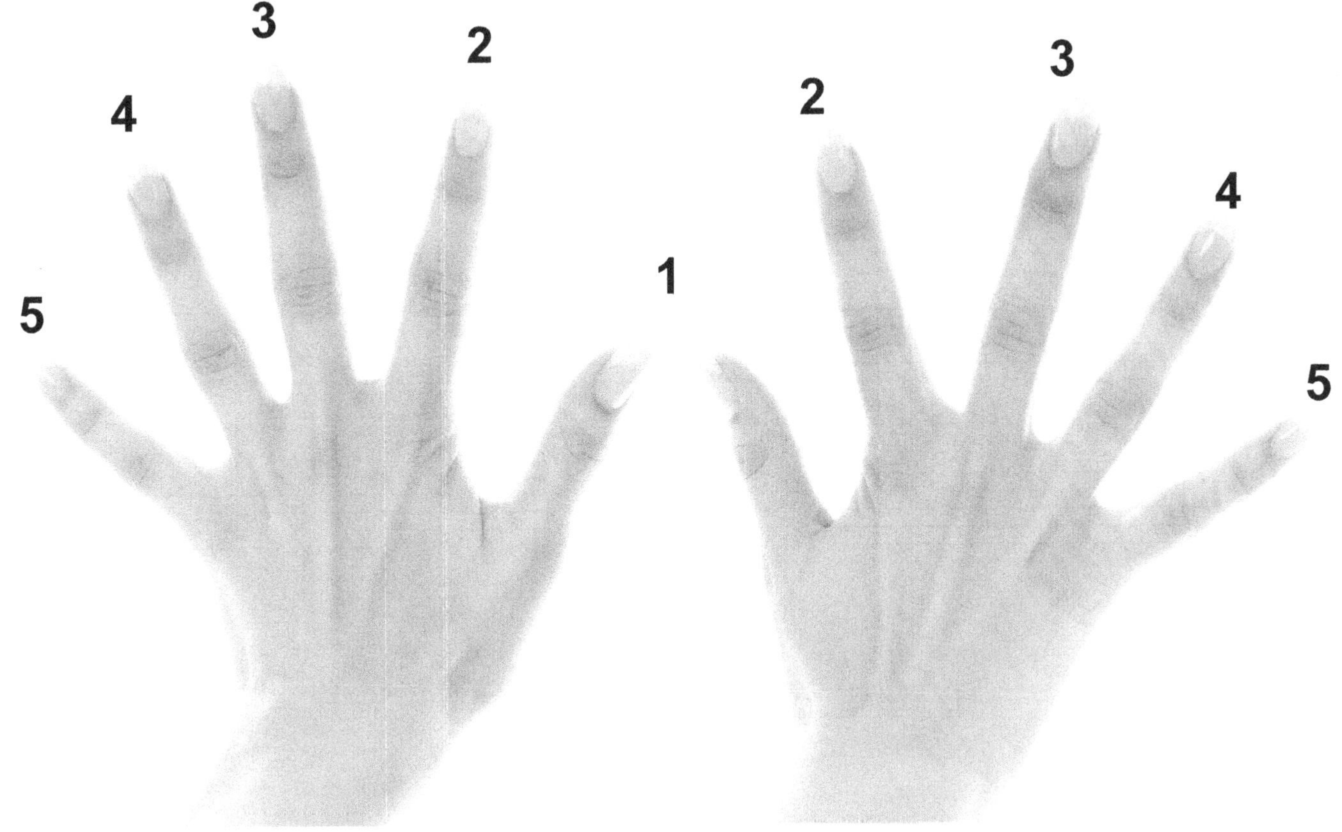

51

52

53

54

55

56

57

58

59

60

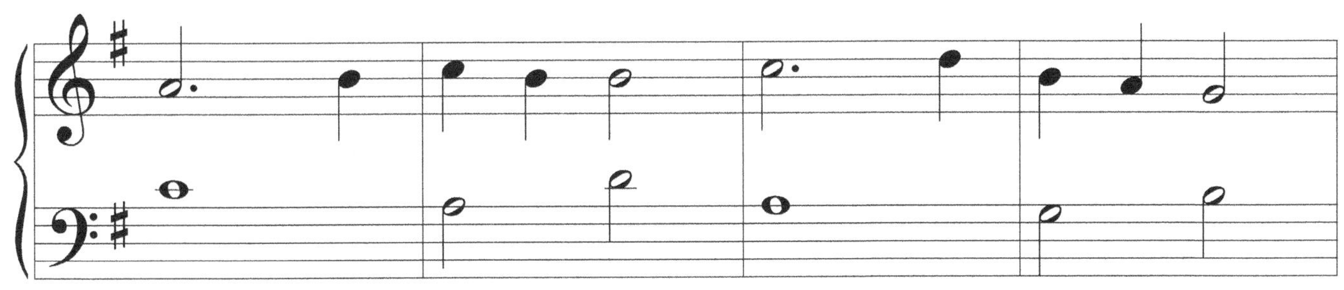

Music Reading Skills for Piano

Level 2

www.RobertAnthonyPublishing.com

Part I:

Reading Studies

This section contains 40 reading studies in the key families of C Major, F Major, and G Major. These studies are all in 4/4 time and the rhythms are kept very simple, placing the emphasis on pitch and fingering.

Since this is a "Level Two" book, it is assumed that the student is aware of the locations of the notes on the keyboard.

1

1

3

2

3

4

5

6

7

8

9

10

11

12

13

14

15

16

18

19

20

21

22

2

mp

4

mf

f

3
f
5
mp
mf
p
mf

24

25

26

2
mf
5
1
5
2
5
2
1
2
2
p
4
1
5
1
f
5
4
p
4
5
4

28

29

5
mp
3
1
1
1
f
5
1
2
1
2
1
2
4
3
2
p
5
5

31

32

33

4
4
f
5
1
1
1
mp
4
f
5
1
2

35

36

3
p
5
1
1
mf
5
4
p
3
2
1
1

1
5
mf
3
4
1 3
1
5
4
p
1
2
5
2
4
1 3
1
2 4
f
1

1
2
p
5
5
1
3
2
mf
4
2 1
1
2
p
4
1
2
5
1

40

Part II:

Putting the Skills to Work

This section contains repertoire from the Baroque, Classic, and Romantic Periods.

Some different time signatures are used as well as some new rhythmic figures. If you are unfamiliar with them, they are thoroughly covered in Rhythm and Meter for All Musicians from Robert Anthony Publishing.

Andante

Turk

Scherzo

Gurlitt

Etude

Czerny

Play both hands one octave higher than written

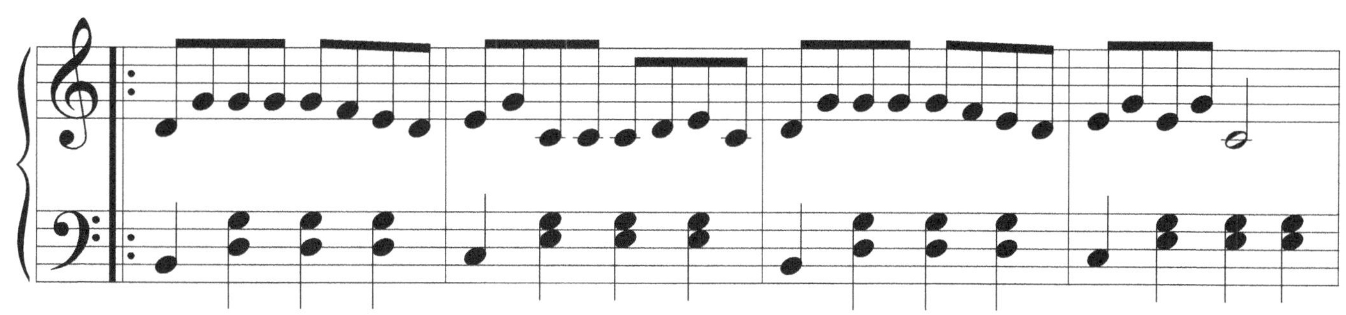

Etude

Czerny

Play both hands one octave higher than written.

Etude

Waltz

Diabelli

2
4
2
5
5
2

Minuet

L. Mozart

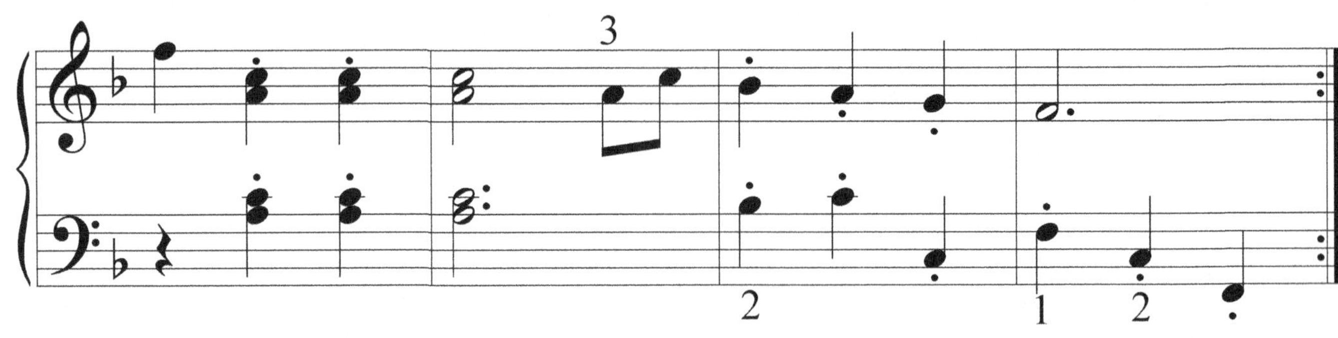

Summer Song

Liadov

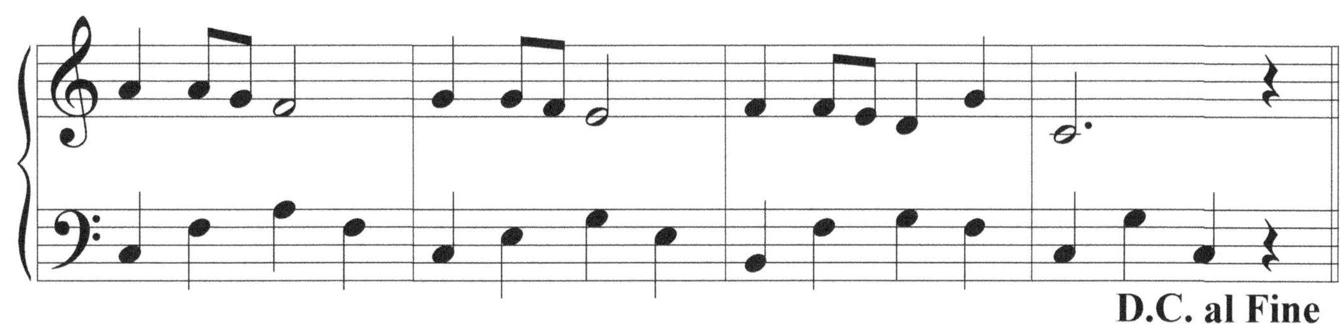

Song Without Words

Köhler

3
1
5
1
5
5
1
4
1
5
1

Allegretto

Giuliani

2
5
1
2
5
1
1
2
1
1
4
2
1
2
3
1
1
1

Sonatina in C
First Movement

Latour

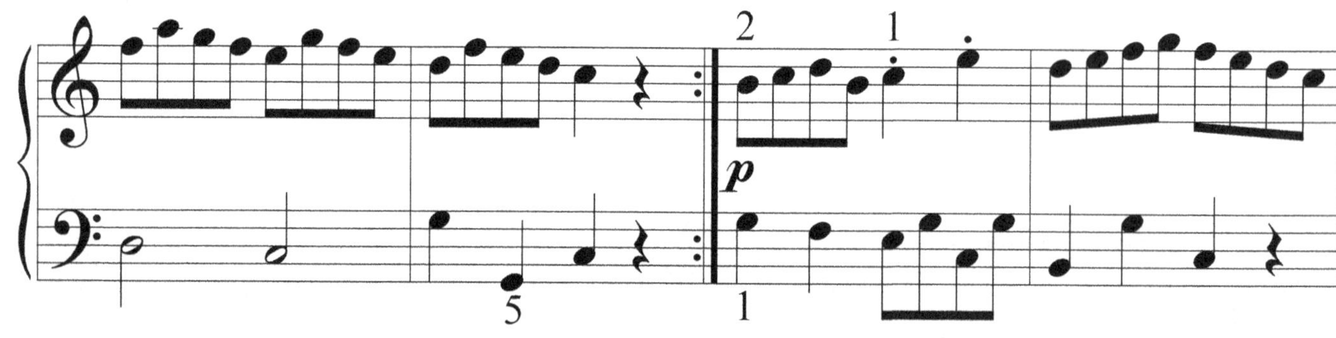

2
1
a tempo
rit.
mp
mf
f

Andante in C

Sor

Minuet in G major

J.S. Bach

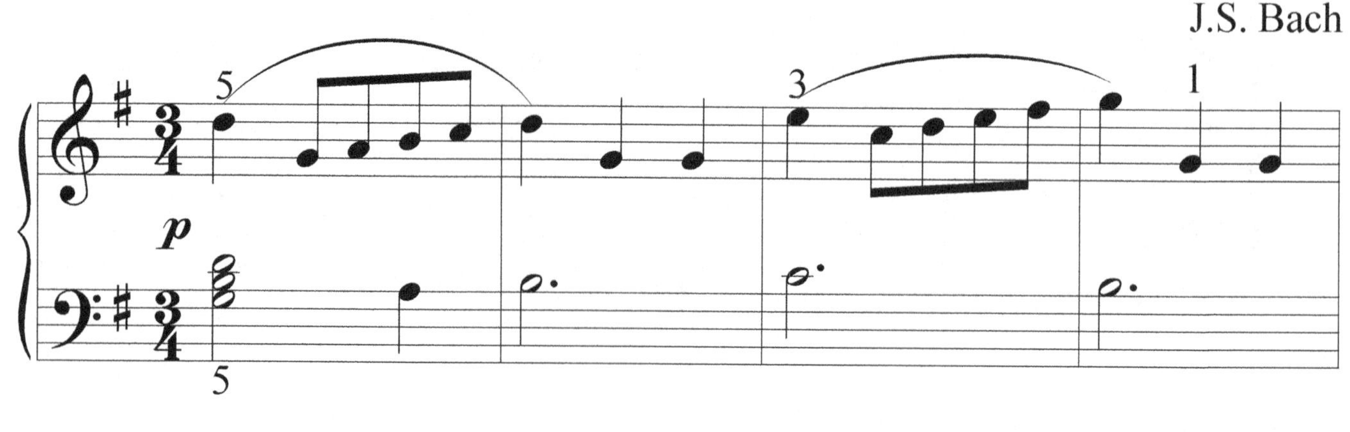

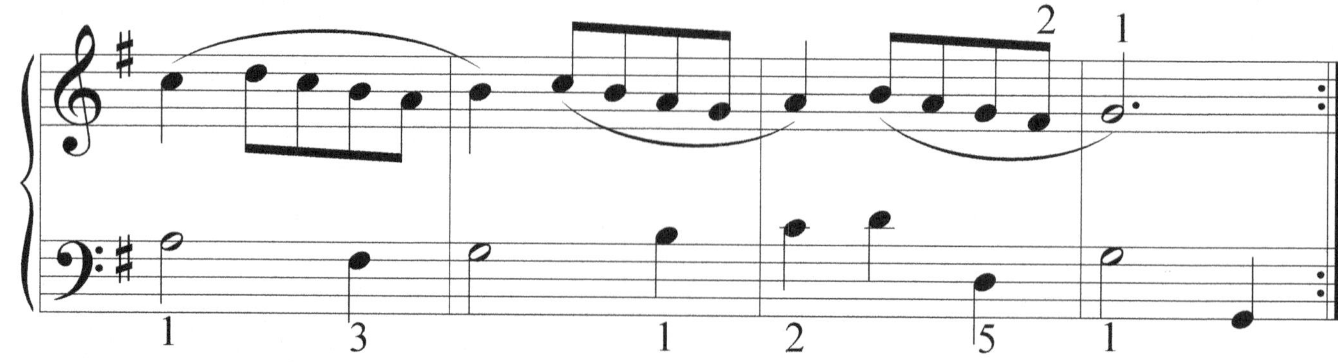

mf

Minuet

L. Mozart

D.C. al Fine

Music Reading Skills for Piano

Level 3

www.RobertAnthonyPublishing.com

Part I:

Reading Studies

This section contains 35 reading studies in the major keys of C, G, F, D, Bb, A, Eb, and their relative minor keys. These studies are all in 4/4 time and the rhythms are kept very simple, placing the emphasis on pitch and fingering.

Since this is a "Level Three" book, it is assumed that the student is aware of the locations of the notes on the keyboard.

1

2

3

4

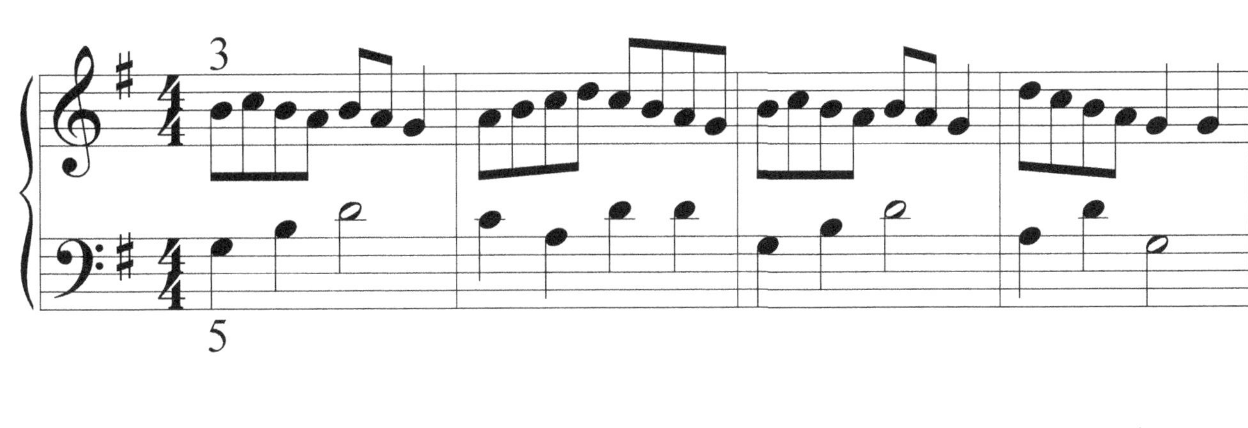

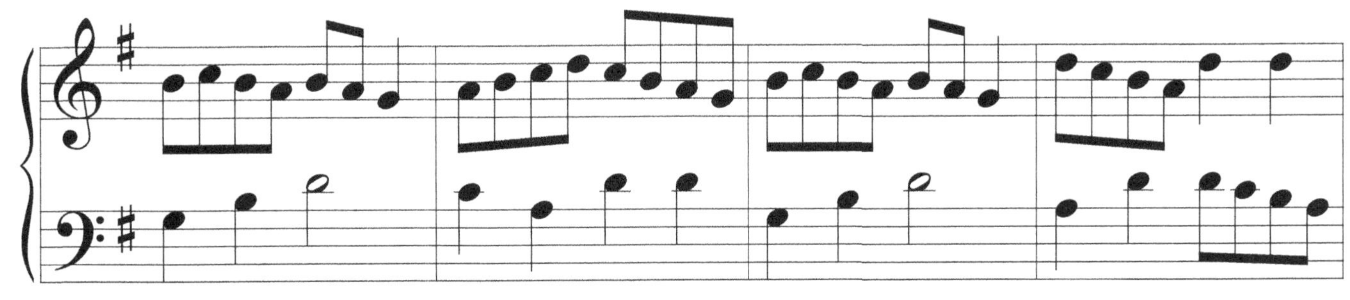

5

6

7

8

9

10

11

12

13

14

15

16

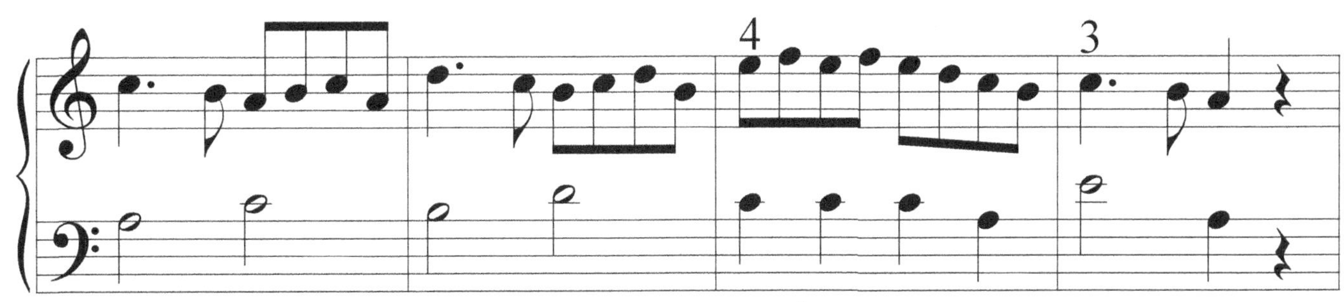

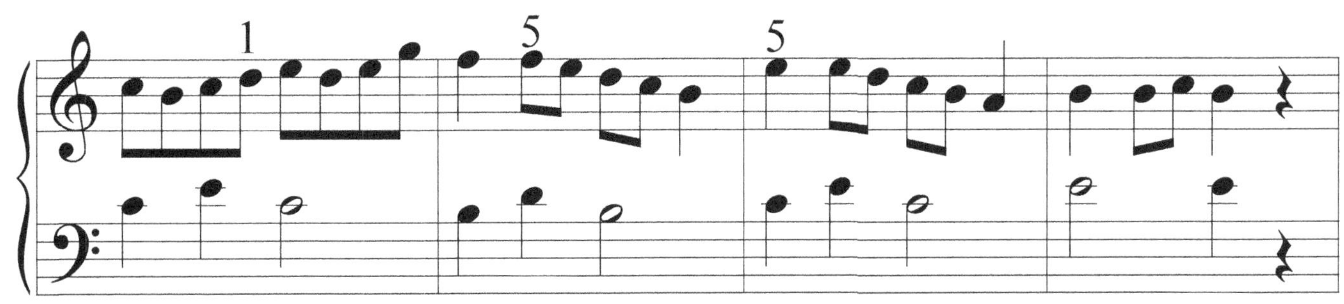

17

18

19

20

21

22

23

24

25

26

27

28

29

30

31

32

33

34

35

Part II:

Putting the Skills to Work

This section contains repertoire from the Baroque, Classic, and Romantic Periods.

Some different time signatures are used as well as some new rhythmic figures. If you are unfamiliar with them, they are thoroughly covered in Rhythm and Meter for All Musicians from Robert Anthony Publishing.

Minuet in C Major

W.A. Mozart

Rondo

Allegretto

Latour

p
f
p
poco rit. e dim.

Scherzo

Allegretto

Weber

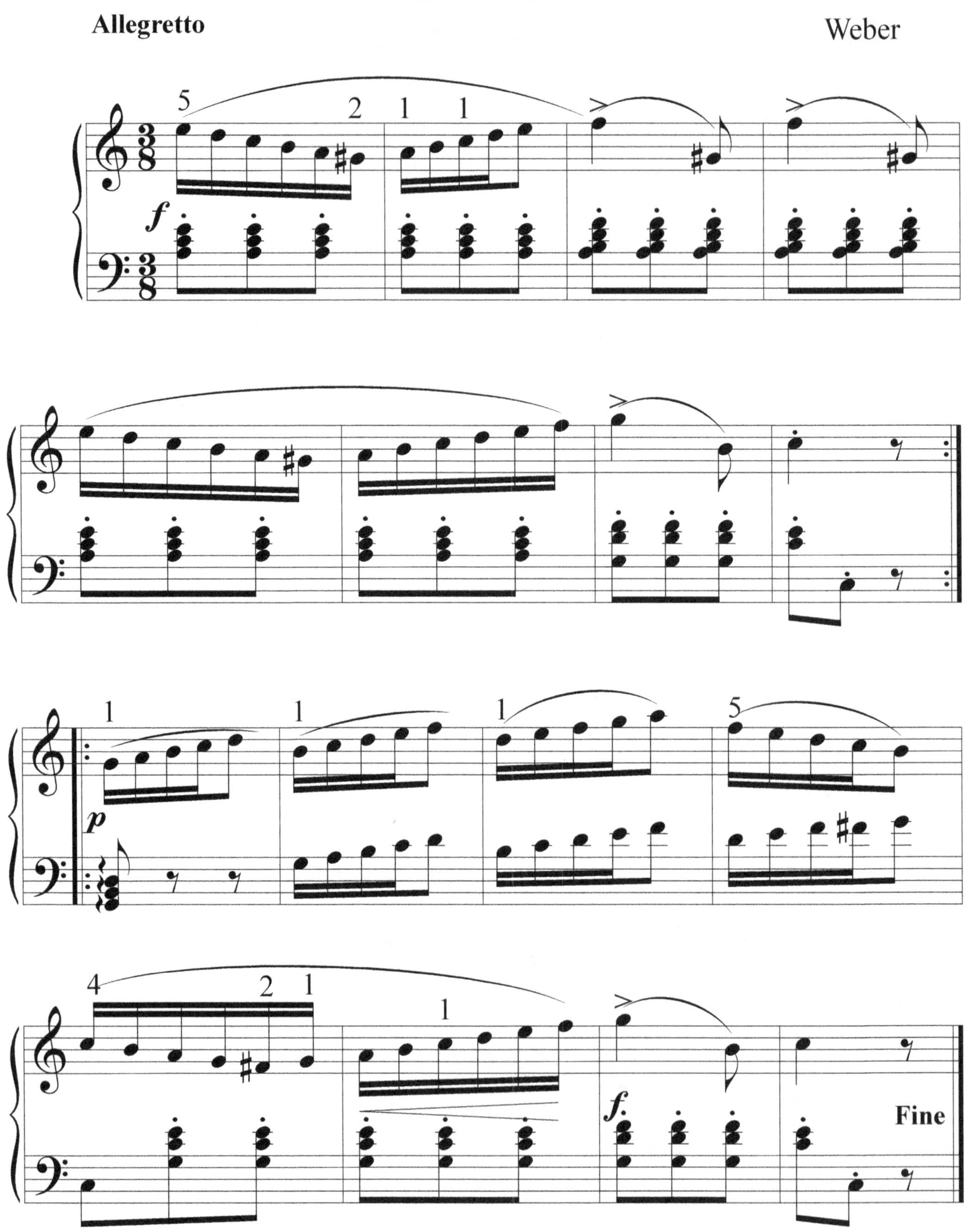

Trio
p
mf
p
D.C. al Fine

Study

Czerny

Etude in A Minor

Moderato

Kohler

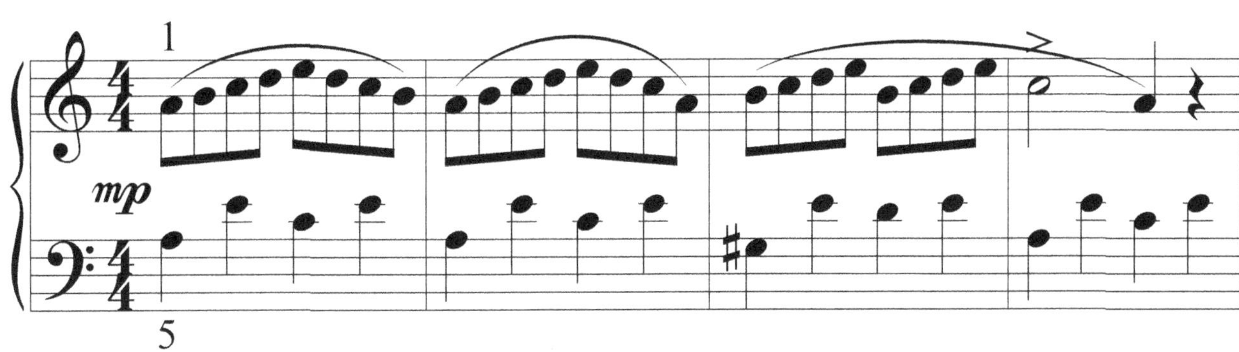

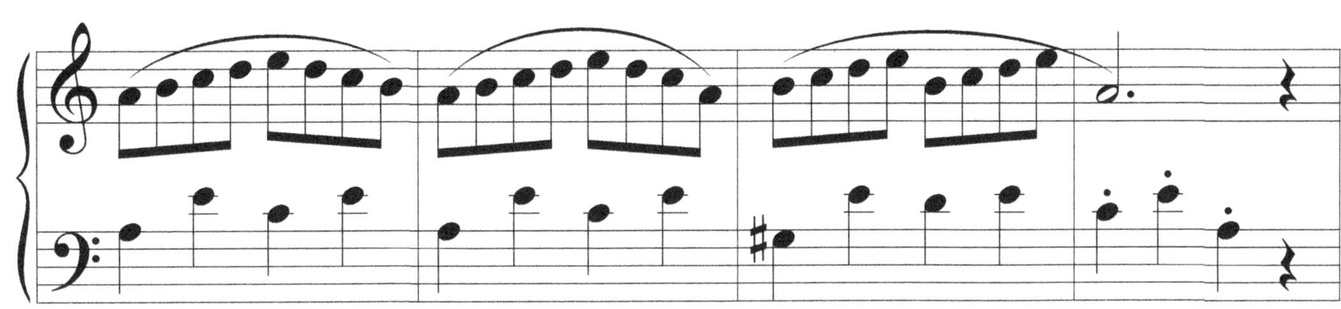

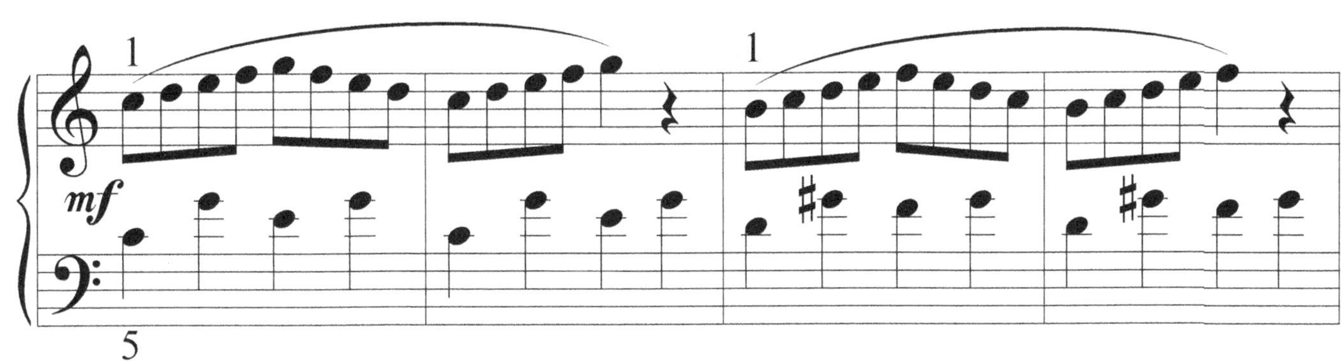

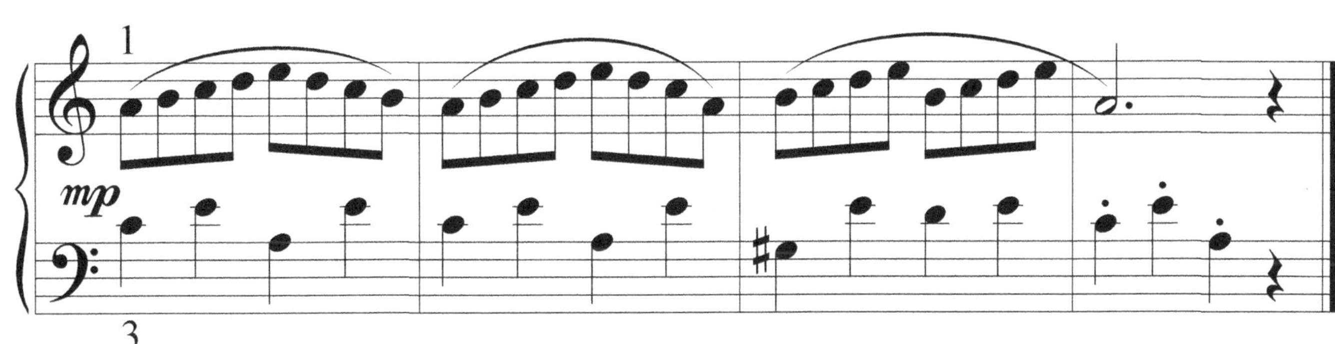

Minuet in G Minor

J.S. Bach

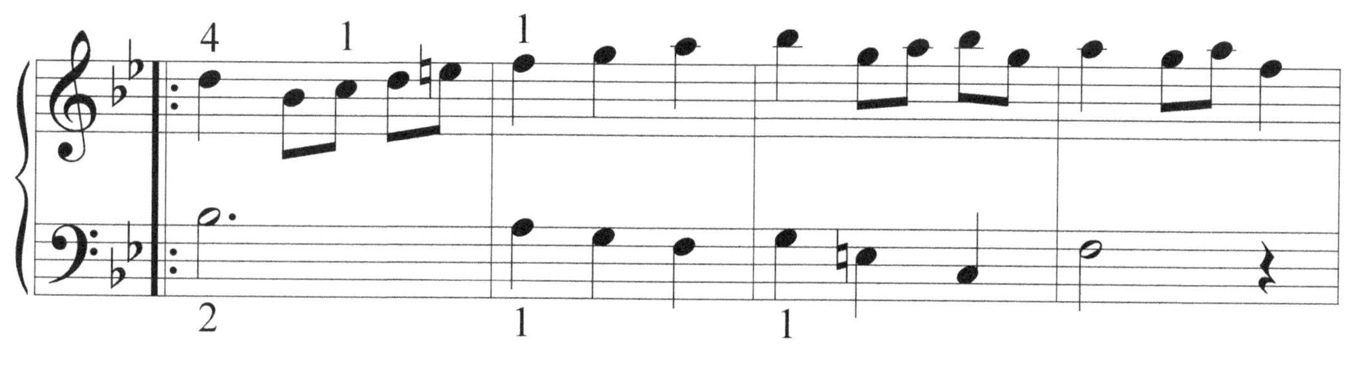
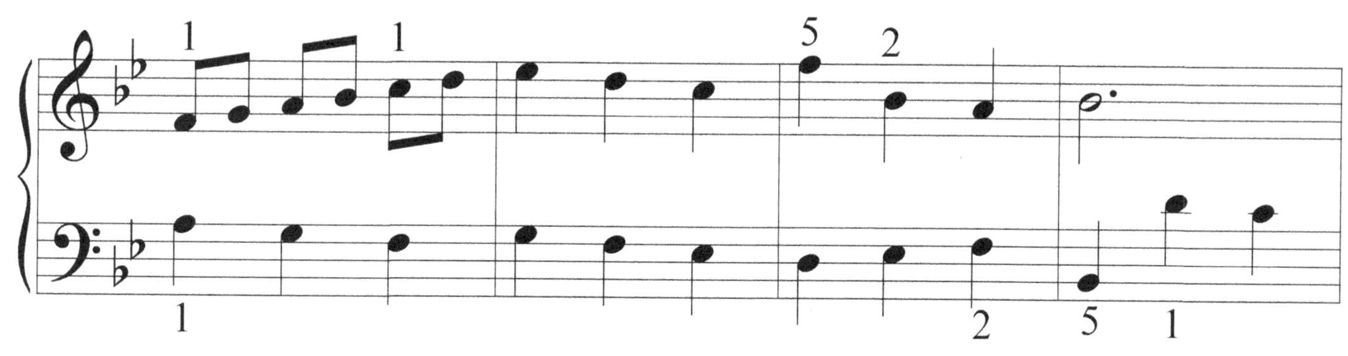
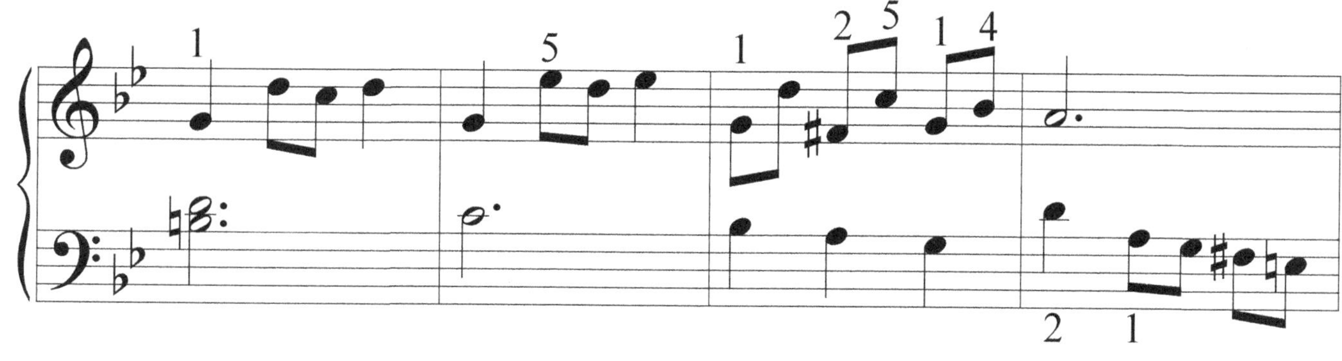

Russian Folk Song

Beethoven

Allegretto

Haydn

Minuet in F Major

Allegretto

W.A. Mozart

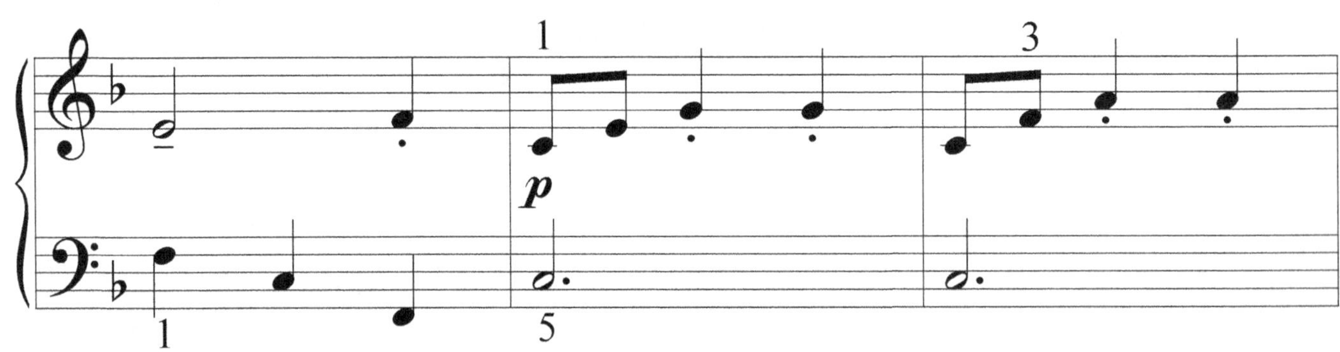

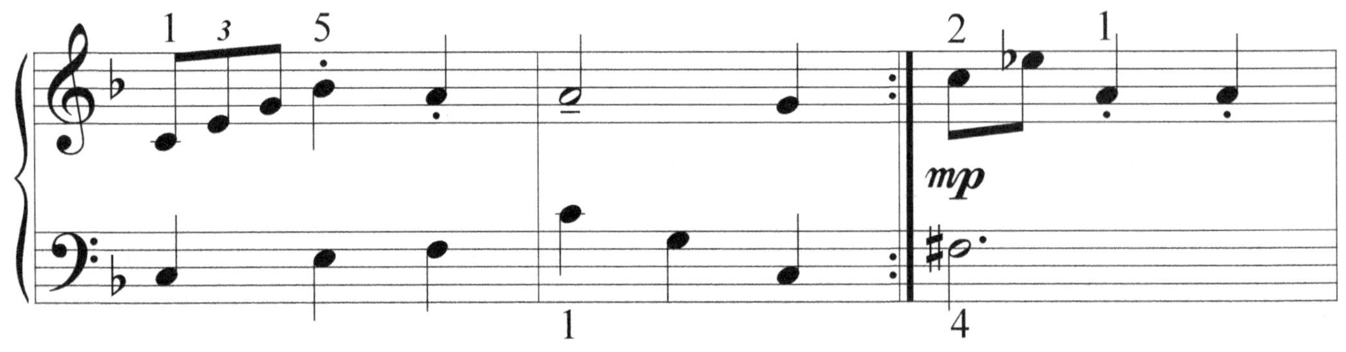

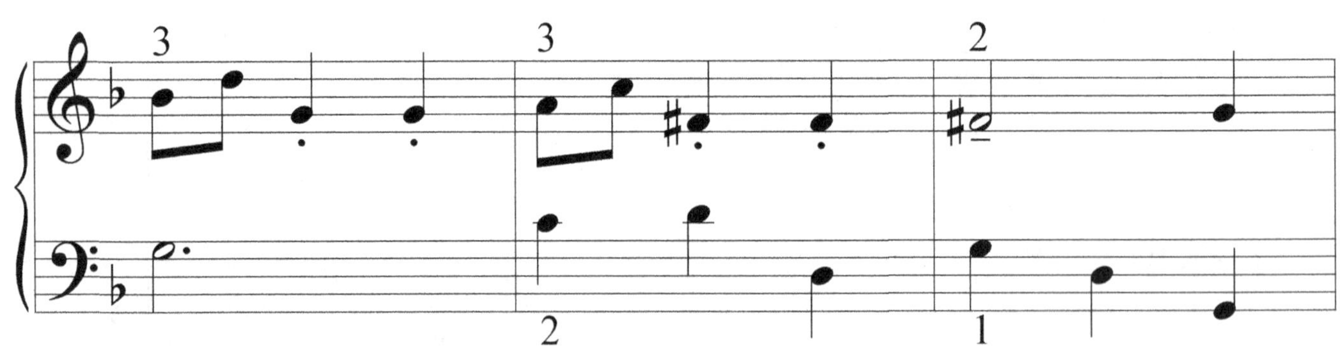

3
3
3
p
4
2
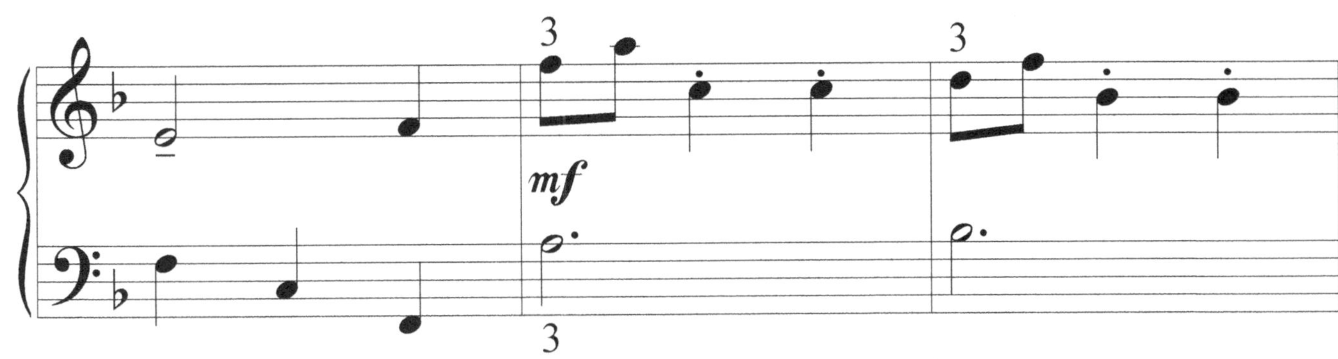
3
3
mf
3

3
3
f
3
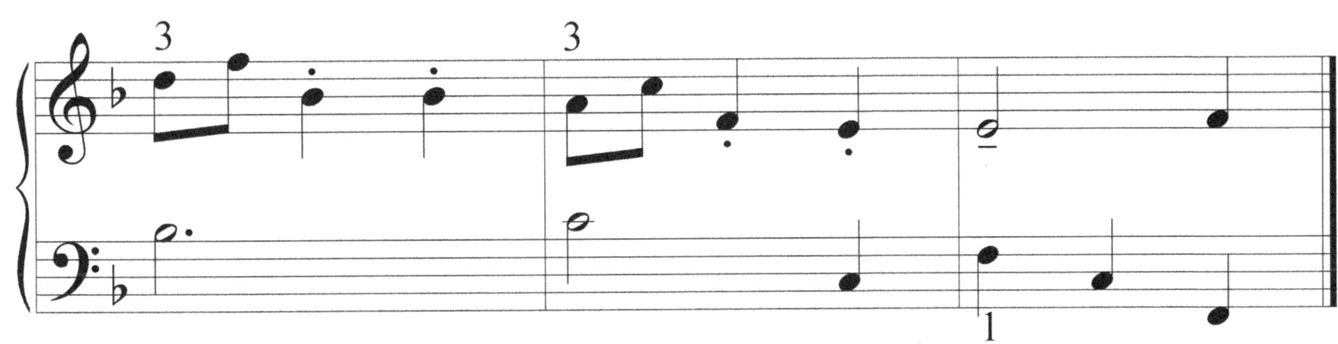
3
3
1

German Dance

Allegretto

Haydn

Pastorale
Andante
C.P.E. Bach

Allegro

A Section

L. Mozart

Waltz in A Major

Schubert

Ecossaise

Beethoven

Allegro

1
2
3
2
3
p
1
2
1
2
mf
1
2
3
p

Made in the USA
Middletown, DE
27 November 2022